50 WAYS

——— TO ———

MOTIVATE

YOUR

BOARD

A Guide For Nonprofit Executives

James A. Donovan

DONOVAN MANAGEMENT INC
Orlando

Illustrated by Victor Davila

DEDICATION

This book is dedicated to my wife, Janet —
soccer mom, chair of our household and loving
partner in life and business who makes it all
worthwhile.

Donovan Management Inc.
P.O. Box 195068
Winter Springs, Florida 32719

Printed in the United States of America

ISBN 0-9639875-2-6

Acknowledgments

This being my second professional book, I am most grateful to the two people who again assisted me in a major way.

My wife, Janet, for her persistence in guiding the production of this book and getting it to press, and my editor and design specialist, Joanne Camilli Griggs, for her excellent editing skills and hard work in making the illustrations fit the copy.

I am also grateful to:

Victor Davila, a talented, recent graduate of the University of Central Florida, for his creative artwork and illustrations that add levity and reinforce many of the lessons of the book.

For their reading of the original manuscript, insightful suggestions for revisions, encouragement over the years and warm friendship, I would like to thank:

• Will Ray, President and CEO of the Palm Beach Cultural Council, West Palm Beach, Florida;

• Georges C. St. Laurent, Jr., CEO for Western Bank, Beaverton, Oregon;

• Betty Duda, Central Florida's philanthropic activist;

• Glenn H. Martin, former Orlando executive.

Over 100 clients of Donovan Management who, by sharing their board-related challenges with me, provided the insight and inspiration to write and share these 50 ways with them and thousands of others.

And to the airline flight attendants, hotel staff and other travel service providers who made it possible for me to write most of the manuscript during frequent travels in the past two years.

James A. Donovan

Foreword

As chief executive officer of Florida's largest local cultural agency since 1982, I wish Jim Donovan's newest book had been available to me back when I first began. I second every motion he has made for executive directors in motivating and managing volunteer boards. There are fifty kernels of truth here, every one worth using. I'll also use "50 Ways To Motivate Your Board" in my capacity as President of Florida Philanthropy, as Jim and I and our Florida colleagues build and motivate our statewide board.

I've known Jim Donovan for nearly twenty years now. While in transit from North Carolina to a permanent position in Florida, I worked for Jim when he directed the University of Central Florida Foundation fund-raising program in Orlando. Over the years, we have always stayed in touch. It has been exciting for me to watch him grow professionally, especially in his commitment to research and writing about timely topics important to all of us who advance philanthropy. I believe a true professional passes along his best ideas. A committed one, writes them down.

Jim's first book, "Take The Fear Out Of Asking For Major Gifts" is itself a major gift to fund-raising literature. It's also helped thousands of volunteers and staff overcome their anxiety in asking for money. If you haven't read it, I strongly urge you to do so.

Like Jim, I believe the two greatest challenges facing nonprofit executives are competing for a shrinking pool of available volunteer leaders and, once recruited to your board, motivating them to achieve the organization's mission. In simple straightforward words, with concrete, personal examples, Jim tells a compelling story every nonprofit executive should hear. Board members are our most valuable asset. Their care and feeding is as important to meeting our mission as anything we do.

My only regret in reading this book is wishing I had written it myself. However, my good friend and colleague has done it for me. Thanks, Jim!

William E. Ray
President and CEO
Palm Beach County Cultural Council
West Palm Beach, Florida
May, 1997

Preface

If you are . . .
the chairperson of the board,
executive director,
vice president,
or director of development
of a nonprofit agency/organization/
institution
or if you aspire to one of these positions,
this book is for you.

Its purpose is quite simply, to be a guide to motivate your board of directors. Unlike my first book, "Take The Fear Out Of Asking For Major Gifts," which was a serious commentary on asking for money, this book is light-hearted. It's designed to be a quick read to relax you with some humorous illustrations and real-life anecdotes along the way.

These 50 ways represent over twenty-five years of trial and error experiences as a staff development officer at half-a-dozen institutions and the last eleven years as a consultant to some 100 clients. Having spent my entire professional life in philanthropy, I've learned a lot, and I have taken an inventory of those ideas that work best when it comes to working with governing boards.

More importantly, I believe consultants and other professionals should pass on the best of what they've learned by writing it down. After all, this business of nonprofit management and fund raising gets more challenging by the day. With over one million nonprofit organizations promoting their causes today, the competition for the philanthropic dollar is formidable.

Being a consultant in philanthropy, you will not be surprised to learn that ninety percent of the time when a prospective client invites me to make a proposal for service, it's for **fund-raising** services. What will surprise you is that over fifty percent of these requests are for the wrong service. Many nonprofit executives fail to recognize their problems today. They think they need more money, when, in fact, they really need a better run organization. And, that must start with a board of directors which is highly motivated.

In order to motivate a nonprofit board of directors, you must first engage them. If they are not engaged, you have a ship without a rudder. "50 Ways" attempts to provide you with some tactics, steps and strategies to engage your board in the pursuit of your mission.

Admittedly, some of the methods are unconventional. For example, the suggestion of popping popcorn prior to a board meeting. Others, like conducting a board retreat, are serious suggestions at planning for the future. The 50 ways are not in any specific order. You don't have to start with the first "way," and progress or build on each consecutive one.

It is my hope that as you flip, scan, and read these pages that you will find many new ways to motivate yourself and your board of directors.

James A. Donovan

Five Suggestions For Getting The Most Out Of This Book

1 Resist the temptation to drive and "read it" at the same time.

2 Don't put it on your bookshelf. Keep it somewhere on your desk where it will be noticed by directors of your board. They'll get the hint.

3 Turn the pages and stop on impulse. Whichever of the 50 ways you land on, try that one.

4 Try what you perceive as the most unconventional of the 50 ways first. Why not? What have you got to lose?

5 Place this book under your pillow at night before you go to sleep. You'll be motivated in the morning.

1 Ask Directors About Their Expectations. Don't Worry. They'll Tell You.

The first step in motivating your board of directors is knowing their motivation for serving your organization and their expectations. Directors of nonprofit organizations have their own motivations and expectations about the organization they govern. For some, keeping a budget out of the red is their prime concern. For others, building their resumes may be a prime

concern. Quality programs or fund raising may be both an expectation and a motivation. Uncovering these answers is one way you can actually motivate your board of directors. Never assume you know or understand the answers. Find out for sure by meeting with each director. Ask these basic questions:

• Why did you volunteer your time to serve on this board?

• What expectations do you have for our organization? What would you like to see accomplished?

• How will the staff and I know if we have met your expectations?

•How will you evaluate the board's effectiveness in meeting these expectations?

• How can the staff and I assist you in meeting these expectations?

Each question is purposely direct and should elicit a direct response. The answer to the first question will tell you what motivates the director. The second question attempts to discover the criteria by which success for the organization is defined. The last question, "How can I assist you?" is the motivator. This presumes that the director needs and wants your help. Most volunteers will accept an offer of assistance.

You should also use this occasion to demonstrate your charm, wit, intelligence and enthusiasm for the work of your organization. Your presence alone can be a motivating factor for the director.

Keep in mind that the last thing a director of your board wants to do is your job. However, a director needs help in getting his/her job done.

2 Have A Plan. Write It Down. Distribute It. "It's In My Head" Doesn't Count.

Nothing impresses or inspires directors more than knowing there is a plan (a road map) as to where your organization is headed. Once they have been told of the challenges facing your organization, they want to know what steps are going to be taken to meet them. Directors of your board do not expect to sit idle from one meeting to the next. They want (and deserve) a detailed schedule of activities with deadlines for the completion of major tasks. For example, haven't you had a similar encounter as noted below?

Let's say you're having a board meeting. The newest member of your board asks, "I may be new to this board, but all I keep hearing are a lot of ideas for marketing, fund raising and how we've got to keep costs down. When are we going to agree on our primary concerns and begin making long-term plans so we know where we are headed in the next twelve to twenty-four months?"

Sound familiar? Of course it does, because that's the way most nonprofit organizations operate to-day. **Plan for the future.** Not just in your mind, but on paper too so others can read, review and reflect on the plan. This process does make a difference in motivating your board. The plan doesn't have to be elaborate, but well thought out and sensible for your organization, given the situation, circumstances and challenges you face today.

Begin preparing your plan by writing a brief vision statement. Dream a little. Actually, dream a lot! Envision your organization twenty-five years from now, ten years and five years. Imagine what resources — human, financial and physical that are needed to advance your organization. How will these resources affect the approach to carrying out your mission? What problem would be solved (or closer to being solved) for society? How will your work make a difference in the lives of those you serve? As Stephen R. Covey, the best selling author of "The Seven Habits of Highly Effective People," says, "Begin with the end in mind." This ought to help you conjure up images and benchmarks for your organization. Now write them down and dis-tribute the plan.

3 Have A Vision. Most Of Us Enjoy The Benefit Of Sight. Yet, Few Of Us Have Vision.

By "vision" I mean the ability to contemplate the future and write a statement of what we envision. A vision statement for a nonprofit organization should not be confused with a mission statement. The mission statement explains your ultimate purpose. The vision statement describes what you "see" your organization becoming down the road. Remember how former President George Bush was criticized during the 1992 presidential election for not having a vision? He became sensitive about this issue and referred to it as "the vision thing." His advisers kept telling him the American people expected him to define where he saw the country heading in the future. The result was a vision for "a kinder, gentler nation." As it turned out, Bill Clinton's vision of a stronger economy was the vision the American people wanted to hear.

Just as we expect our elected officials to have a vision for the country, nonprofit constituencies expect a vision that challenges and inspires everyone involved to reach for lofty goals.

I particularly like the vision statement of the YMCA in Orlando, Florida: "Our vision is to be the Central Florida leader in prevention and development programs for children and families, and a leader in community development, bringing community resources to bear on social problems."

I also like their mission statement: "The purpose of this association shall be to help develop Christian values and improve the quality of life in Central Florida by involving individuals and families in programs that develop spirit, mind and body."

Dr. Martin Luther King beautifully articulated his vision for America in his famous "I Have A Dream" speech. President John F. Kennedy had a vision of putting a man on the moon. Clara Barton envisioned an international agency to assist victims of war and natural disasters. The Founder of Federal Express had the foresight of a package delivery system that guaranteed overnight delivery anywhere in the world.

> **"Leadership is the special quality which enables people to stand up and pull the rest of us over the horizon."**
>
> **— James L. Fisher**

Nonprofit agencies exist for three purposes — to aid people, pets/animals and the planet. An enthusiastic, well-written vision statement can work wonders in rallying volunteers and donors to the cause.

# Conduct A Board Retreat. Create Your Own Captive Audience.

Today's information society makes it possible for all of us to communicate faster and more often. As a consequence, more and more people are competing for our attention. With electronic mail, facsimile machines, personal pagers and cellular telephones, we find ourselves more accessible than ever. We can no longer say, "I can't wait until I leave this office today and get away from these phones. They won't be able to get to me." The main consequence of this accessibility is that almost every message intended for us is both urgent and important. Or, seemingly so.

In our busy world today, none of us can be "on the run" and focused on anything other than being on the run. We must work hard at not only getting a person's attention, but keeping it. Increasingly, I find myself saying to people, "that sounds like an important matter requiring serious discussion. Let's set a date and time when we can talk about it in depth."

When working with your board of directors, you must save the real important, big issues for serious discussion and when you have their full and undivided attention. The best way, short of kidnapping each director separately, is to commit to a retreat for the board of directors. By my own definition to clients, it's a retreat provided it's held 35 miles or more from the office in a quiet, comfortable setting.

Your retreat should be held for a minimum of one-and-a-half days or a full weekend. More is even better. The key to a successful retreat is planning it with the end result in mind as your foremost objective. In this case, the end result is to create a sense of ownership among your board for the mission, goals and action plan that will result from the retreat. This building of ownership is in itself the highest form of motivation for any board. Also, retreats give board members an opportunity to break bread together — which increases the trust level when they get to know one another.

Often, when I recommend board retreats to my clients, I experience a lot of resistance, mostly in the form of excuses as to why a retreat won't work. The main reason always goes something like this, "If we can't get the directors to attend our board meetings on a regular basis, why would they attend a retreat for two days?" To which I reply, "Maybe one of the reasons your board attendance is poor is because your board members don't feel like there is any grand plan." More often than not the response is, "You're right. Maybe now is the time to create that

plan."

Here are five steps you should take in planning your retreat:

1. First, identify the benefits of the retreat. Show how your organization, the board of directors, the staff, and those you serve will benefit.

> "The most effective servants are those who persuade others to go with them and who have learned to work in teams."
>
> — Robert K. Greenleaf

2. Write these benefits down and review them with your board chair.

3. Ask the board chair to make the idea of a retreat an agenda item for the next board meeting and invite him to personally sell the idea to the entire board.

4. Do your homework ahead of time. Estimate the cost of the retreat, three possible locations, names of possible facilitators, proposed schedule, recreation opportunities, such as golf or tennis, and transportation and lodging arrangements. Answer questions about the details of the retreat when they arise in the board meeting.

5. Summarize all arrangements and send each board member a letter from the chair announcing all of the details about the retreat.

5 Distribute The Post-Retreat Plan.

"This weekend discussion has been most helpful, but when are we going to quit talking and get something down on paper?" Surely, you will hear this remark from a director before the conclusion

of your retreat if the ideas discussed aren't summarized in writing.

Take time during and after the retreat to summarize the board's discussions and the plans they made. This will keep the enthusiasm going during the post-retreat period. By preparing and distributing a written summary of the retreat, your board will know you are serious about the planning process. You will soon see how the planning process focuses your board on setting goals for your organization. Without clear organizational goals, executive directors run the risk of having their board members meddling in the organization's day-to-day operations.

6 Assign Each Director A Task. If Directors Are Idle, They'll Meddle.

One of the staff positions I held was at the University of Central Florida in Orlando. Like many fast growing public universities, the university has a separate fund-raising entity, the UCF Foundation. When I arrived on the scene, there were 50 directors on the foundation board. Much to my amazement, none had been assigned any duties except the members of the executive committee. I talked to the president of the foundation and suggested that we ask each director to serve on a standing committee. To my delight and amazement, he said, "Jim, we're not going to ask them. I'm going to tell them by appointing each one to a committee."

When I told the president of the university about the appointment, he responded with: "You did what?" He was concerned about disgruntled directors complaining to him about such a "Don't ask them; tell them what to do" approach.

In the end, no one was offended. In fact, several directors were pleased to be given an assignment. The lesson learned was — sometimes board members want to be told what is expected of them.

You might be wondering: "How does this square with the first suggestion in this book, to ask direc-

tors about their expectations?" During my interviews with the directors, it was clear they hadn't
given much thought as to what their expectations were for the university's foundation. At
least, they weren't able to articu-
late them. So I told the president
of the foundation what I had
learned, and he decided the time
had come to tell our directors
what was expected of them. He
obviously knew most of the directors well enough that he was
confident he could assert his
leadership. This would have
been quite risky for both of us
had I not interviewed each director beforehand. As it turned out,
it was the right task at the right
time. You may be facing a similar
situation. If you are, be cautious
with this approach as it could
backfire if your board president
isn't respected.

7 Prepare A Job Description For Each Director And Train Them.

A job description for a volunteer director is a necessity. Volunteer leaders want to know about the specific duties they are to carry out in the performance of their responsibility as a director of your organization. Job descriptions are like a covenant between volunteers and staff. The volunteer freely agrees to perform specific tasks (without compensation) in return for staff support, recognition and advancement in the organization.

I subscribe to Peter Drucker's job description for directors of nonprofit boards as explained in his book, "Managing The Nonprofit Organization." Drucker says that directors serve four functions. These are as follows:

Governors — They govern the work of the organization in their role as policymakers.

Ambassadors — They spread goodwill about the organization among those they come in contact with.

Consultants — They provide their expertise to other board members and especially to the organization's chief executive officer.

Sponsors — They underwrite the work of the

organization through their personal or corporate financial support.

I encourage my clients to use Drucker's model as a preamble to their job descriptions. The remainder of the job description should include the essential elements this example shows:

1. Statement of Responsibility

Public Relations Chair: To provide expertise and direction on the planning and execution of the organization's public relations program so as to create a positive image within the community.

2. Duties/Tasks: To provide access to key media sources. To serve as organizational spokesperson during major events. To nurture and develop strong ties with the media.

3. Reporting: Reports to board chair

4. Supervision: Other committee members and indirectly the staff, particularly the public relations officer.

6. Evaluation: Annually by committee.

Keep the job description to one typed page. Upon appointment of the Public Relations Chair, review the job description with the chair. At the end of the chair's term, revise/update the job description.

Finally, train your board. Directors need orientation about your mission, goals, policies, procedures. Conduct formal board training for new members. For the best orientation program around, I suggest that used by the American Red Cross. It's superb. Give your local chapter a call.

8 Chart A Course Of Upward Mobility For Each Director. It's Up Or Out.

Each director must have a sense of where he or she is headed within your organization. A time investment should not be viewed as an occasional involvement with your organization, but rather a charted course whereby each one is exposed to a variety of meaningful experiences that broaden his or her skill and expertise as a director of a nonprofit organization.

The business section of any major newspaper in the country has stories about directors of for-profit companies. Oftentimes, it's noted that the recently appointed director serves or has served on other corporate boards. Unlike nonprofit boards, the for-profit boards pay directors for serving. The compensation varies considerably from one company to another, but the goal of the director is the same — increase his or her abilities as a director and simultaneously increase the value of their service/compensation.

Nonprofit directors expect the same. They want to move on to the next board, bigger challenges and perhaps a more prestigious board of directors. By understanding this expectation, a course of upward mobility can and should be set for those directors who desire it. For example, start a new director out on the board's public relations committee, then move him or her to the finance committee and finally to the executive committee. Slowly, the director learns some valuable lessons for the future. This charting keeps your upcoming leaders motivated as they know it's their turn to run things.

9 Ask Your Board Members For Advice.

One criteria for selecting a director to your board is his or her expertise in a particular area, such as finances, public relations or personnel. A common complaint among directors of nonprofit organizations is that their advice is not sought. "We are usually thought of as a rubber stamp," is a common reaction. Over the years, I have found that asking a director for advice makes them feel useful and important. It's also helpful to the nonprofit executive who wishes to validate assumptions on a decision he or she is about to make. I must confess, I've even sought such advice when I knew what I was going to do anyway.

As already noted in number seven, directors should be used as consultants to nonprofit management. After all, you elected them because of their knowledge and expertise. Use them as consultants or else you risk losing them. Seeking advice is not a sign of weakness by an executive director. On the contrary, it shows that you are thinking a matter through, and you're smart enough to engage in consultive management. (Note: I said consultive, not consensus. The latter implies the group is making the decision, not you as executive director.)

Nonprofit executives should tap into the talent and expertise that the directors bring to the board room.

> **"Caring must strengthen into commitment and commitment into action if we are to preserve and nurture one of the greatest forces for rebirth and renewal this nation has — volunteerism."**
>
> **— Marlene Wilson**

10 Challenge Your Board Of Directors To Lead.

Standing board committees are a way of life for nonprofits. Each requires strong leadership to accomplish its goals. Too often, we think leadership from directors as only being at the top — the board chair or the chair-elect. Effective leadership must exist at all levels of your board structure — the executive, finance, development, nominating and audit committees. More importantly, the leaders of these committees must be challenged to lead. Go beyond the usual duties of the chair for

these typical standing committees by being innovative. Encourage committee chairs to raise the horizon of its members by explaining the next level of quality performance for the committee, as well as how that performance is to be measured.

For example, the criteria for successful performance by the finance committee could be as
follows:

- Achieving a 10 percent reduction in operating costs.
- Lowering the cost of fund-raising from 15
cents per dollar to 10 cents.
- Increasing earned income by 2 percent.

Directors of nonprofit boards take great
pride in meeting such goals. This sense of pride
provides momentum and motivation to the
succeeding committee to obtain even better
results.

11 Conduct An Organizational Assessment.

One of the best management exercises a non-profit organization can go through is to retain a consultant to conduct an organizational assessment. The assessment should diagnose the organization's situation. The assessment inventories the organization's resources — personnel, finances, equipment, office space, building and sometimes office location. Ask yourself: "Do we have the tools, talent,

> "The vineyards of philanthropy are pleasant places, and I would hope good men and women will be drawn there. If these vineyards are to thrive and bear their best fruit, they must always have first-class attention."
>
> — **Harold J. Seymour**
> **1894-1986**

supplies and funds to meet our mission?" An assessment can also be done for a particular division or department of a nonprofit organization, such as the development office. Again, the same questions apply.

The benefit of an assessment is that it provides an outside, objective opinion of your organization's pantry. Is the pantry sufficiently stocked? Do you have the main tools and supplies needed to do your job? Is there a particular challenge facing the organization right now? If so, what is the best way to deal with it? For example, your annual giving program has peaked. Is it time to begin a major gifts program? Should the major gifts program include planned gifts? How will you staff the program? What will it cost?

An assessment should not be confused with a management audit, which examines how each staff person spends his or her time relative to their stated job descriptions. The assessment is a great tool in getting the board's attention and setting the agenda for an in-depth discussion of the resources needed in the future, such as a major or planned giving program as noted above.

"... because I am having fun."

— Georges C. St. Laurent, Jr.,
describing why he gave so
generously to the President's Circle
Dinner at the University of
Central Florida.

12 Find A Model Board Of A Similar Nonprofit.

This technique has served my clients well over the years. I constantly hear the same complaint from nonprofit executives: "How can I convince my board that an agency like ours can be successful?" Too often, directors of nonprofit boards become cynical and negative. They can develop a defeatist attitude, especially those who have served too long. Say, for example, that your agency is the Humane Society. The board members think that only those who love pets will contribute to the society, provided they hear about the need for adoptions in the local media. When you explain to the board that more individual giving is possible, they just don't hear you.

Find another Humane Society in your region that has a successful fund-raising program and ask them about their secrets to success. Invite their board or fund-raising chair to one of your meetings to talk about how the fund-raising program is run. Board members will get the message. If you want to be equally successful, you can by following the same strategies. This works because you are comparing similar agencies and circumstances and because an outsider is communicating the message in a non-threatening, objective manner.

13 Get To Know Your Directors. Take An Interest In What They Do.

Nonprofit executives usually meet with their board of directors during normal business hours. This doesn't leave much time to get to know your directors socially. Therefore, organize a social event for your board such as a cook-out, dinner party or "business after hours" event. Keep it casual, informal and relaxed. Get to know and appreciate the interests of your directors. You'll be surprised what you can learn. Imagine this encounter:

"I didn't know your daughter was a competitive swimmer and eligible for a college scholarship, Mrs. Thorpe," said the Executive Director.

"Oh, yes," replied Mrs. Thorpe, "Ginny is determined to earn a scholarship to the University of Miami for her swimming ability."

"Where does Ginny train?" the Executive Director asked. "Usually at the YWCA after school," said Mrs. Thorpe.

Now you know something dear to your director's heart. Her daughter is working hard to earn a swimming scholarship. From this moment on, you should scan the sports section of the local newspaper and keep up with Ginny's progress. How did she finish in her last meet? Where does she rank on the team? What are her coaches and the competition saying about her?

Keep notes in your file about further developments in Ginny's life. Look for press coverage in the sports section of your local newspaper, clip and send the articles about Ginny's progress to her mom. At the next meeting of the Board of Directors, be the first to say to Mrs.

"The true source of cheerfulness is benevolence. The soul that perpetually overflows with kindness and sympathy will always be cheerful."

— Parke Godwin
1816-1904

Thorpe, "I noticed Ginny did quite well in that last swim meet."

Undoubtedly, she will reply, "And you were so kind to send that press clipping."

14 Compile and Publish Lists of Names And Watch What Happens.

Every nonprofit organization issues updated reports, such as minutes of meetings, donor honor rolls or membership listings. We all know what happens when these lists are read by directors. They look for their own name first. "Was I listed as a donor? Did they include my $100 gift in the Century Club? Is my name spelled correctly?" Anyone not listed will be conspicuous by his or her absence. You must be tactful in how you do this, but the most important reason for sending out lists is that they embarrass those who haven't been doing their part. "Shame them into it" is a standard practice among volunteers and staff.

15 Have A Policy Requiring Board Members To Give.

"The board must give if it expects others to do so," is a main principle of fund raising. It amazes me just how many boards really believe that someone else should give the money and their only role is to budget it. Equally amazing is the number of executive directors and board chairs who avoid asking their board members to give. Chairs make excuses such as, "We can't do that. We told them when we recruited them to the board that all they had to do was attend a few meetings." Or, "We do have a policy. It's informal. Everyone knows what is expected of him or her." Better yet, how about this one? "Not everyone can afford to make a big gift, so we count in-kind donations and time contributed."

Because of my years as a consultant, I can say unequivocally that those nonprofit institutions that have a "must give" policy are the most successful. I believe in phasing in such policies over a three-year period, unless you know you can get a firm policy approved right away. Here are three suggestions for gradually making this important change:

(a) Adopt a policy of "Give or get off." This is a good beginning for those boards that have the highest degree of resistance. Essentially, each director is challenged to give according to his or her capacity or resign. This works well with small emerging social service agencies that have a difficult time recruiting high-level corporate leaders because these directors are very often more motivated to serve based on personal reasons. For example, a director may have a child who is diabetic; therefore, serving on the board of the American Diabetes Association is a natural motivation. So too is giving a gift

to find a cure for diabetes, if you have the funds.

(b) Challenge directors of the board to join a particular gift club level, such as the Founders Club, which may require an annual gift of $500. If you don't have such a club, start one and challenge the board of directors to be the charter members. Then, when you have full board participation, go out and challenge others to join. Gift clubs provide status and recognition. These clubs work, provided they are marketed as being special or exclusive.

(c) Hire a consultant to conduct a board assessment. The assessment should review the level of giving by the board over the last five years and evaluate the board members' potential for giving. It doesn't take long to figure out what the board can give collectively when their peers are evaluating the potential for giving. The consultant's assessment will point out the need for improvement and provide recommendations for increasing the level of giving by board members. By using a consultant, you can incorporate a change in a more objective manner because the stimulus for change is subtly coming from outside the organization.

Once your board giving policy is underway, you will see a more energized board. The board will be proud of its giving and more committed than before the policy was in effect.

16 Emphasize The Values Your Organization Stands For.

The big national debate today is over values. Family values, moral values and religious values. People will be drawn to your organization not only because of the work you do, but also because of the values you represent. This shared interest in values is a powerful common bond for motivating members of your board.

For example, The Right To Life Movement, originally started and perceived as a Catholic cause, has blossomed into an ecumenical movement with representatives from all religions. Congressman Newt Gingrich's Contract With America captured the interest of middle America by stressing an agenda that represented the values of millions of Americans. Amnesty International has rallied citizens worldwide to join the fight for human rights for the politically oppressed.

Obviously, these are examples of worldwide movements. However, local movements exist in such organizations as the Parent Teachers Association, Friends of the Library and the Humane Society. Too often nonprofit executives stress governance or fund-raising as the main duty of a director.

When you stress the values your organization represents, you will be pleasantly surprised to see how enthusiastically a nominee to your board may respond the next time you invite him or her to serve on your board of directors. For example, suppose you are recruiting a business executive to serve on the board of directors of a Catholic high school. The executive isn't Catholic, but he is an influential person in your community with a child enrolled in the school. You can begin by asking him if discipline, quality education, religious studies and hard work are things he values. More than likely, he will say these are the reasons he chose this school for his son. Thus, you clearly are on common ground in regard to shared values.

17 Have An Elevator Speech And Use It To Support Your Case.

At your next board of directors meeting, try this exercise. Ask each director to write a statement that answers these four questions:

• Where has our organization been? Its history — milestones achieved.

• Where is our organization today? Its present competitive status.

• Where does our organization want to be in the future? Its potential.

• What investment is required to get there? The financial investment needed to achieve its potential.

Initially, this exercise will result in a short essay, which is fine. However, go back and have the board members cut it down to a 90-second "elevator speech." I call it an elevator speech because you never know when you will be on an elevator and the head of the local community foundation joins you and says, "Hello, judging from your bulging brief case, you're on your way to make a presentation. What does Save The Earth Do?" You respond by giving your elevator speech, covering the main points in your written exercise. Print the elevator speech on a card and take it with you wherever you go. Of course, you don't have to be on an elevator to use your elevator speech. Use it in all of your meetings, appointments or presentations.

When writing your case, emphasize the solutions your organization has for solving a problem, rather than emphasizing the problem itself. For example, years ago emergency relief agencies learned that showing a hungry child throughout an entire television commercial made the viewer feel sad. Viewers would change the channel to block out the misery. Today these commercials devote only a few seconds to the problem — a hungry child. The remainder of the ad shows a smiling, happy face. Thus, the viewer sees how his gift can make a difference.

18 Create A Volunteer Calendar and Hand It Out.

There may be 365 days in a year, but there are less than 100 days per year on the volunteer calendar. Most board members assume that they have a full year to accomplish their goals. Not so. Take a good look at any calendar and examine it month by month. You can exclude Mondays and Fridays, as volunteers are getting their week underway at the beginning of the week and winding up at the end of the week. That leaves Tuesday, Wednesday and Thursday. At best, you will be lucky to get two and a half days of volunteer time, on average, out of this three-day spread. If you don't agree with this analysis, then add in holidays, such as Presidents' Day, Martin Luther King's Birthday, Super Bowl Weekend, Valentine's Day, St. Patrick's Day, religious feast days, April 15th Tax Day, May graduations, Mother's Day, Father's Day, June weddings, Fourth of July, August vacations, September college homecomings, Labor Day, Halloween, Thanksgiving and, of course, Christmas. Combine this with other special events by the local Chamber of Commerce, government and businesses and it becomes clear just how few days volunteers have on their remaining calendar.

I encourage clients to prepare a twelve-month calendar that demonstrates to their volunteers and staff just how few days there are each month to accomplish the organization's tasks. For example, in Puerto Rico the American Red Cross began regional phonathons in major cities around the island. The staff planned on having volunteers from each of the five designated cities call annual gift prospects in their respective cities for two consecutive days each month for four months. Not until I made up a volunteer calendar of available volunteer days did the development staff begin to grasp the urgency of getting organized. They thought they had lots of time for planning, organizing and running the phonathons. My calendar calculations showed that they had one-third of the time they originally estimated to run five successful phonathons.

Try this exercise for yourself and share it with your board. It will instill a sense of urgency among them.

19 Appeal To The Board of Directors' Pride.

Colleges and universities are masters at appealing to alumni pride. Imagine a homecoming weekend at Harvard University. Public universities, such as the University of Nebraska, which have won back-to-back national football titles, know something about alumni pride. It's no accident that the development and public relations staff of these institutions fill their publications with reminders of why alumni should be proud of their alma mater.

> **"It is very satisfying not just to send money, or be what I call a checkbook donor, but to get involved with projects."**
> **— Jack Eckerd**

Every nonprofit organization has its own alumni constituency. The Boy Scouts count former President Gerald Ford as an alumnus. Actor Denzel Washington is featured as an alumnus of the Boys Clubs in its advertising campaign. Cancer treatment centers affiliated with major hospitals run ads showing former patients as "Cancer Survivors."

My favorite example is Marymount College, a private women's college in New York. Several years ago, the college ran a full-page ad in "The New York Times" featuring photos of their alumnae. The headline read, "We Put Women In Their Place." The corresponding photos showed alumnae who were surgeons, attorneys, judges, government officials and chief executive officers of major corporations. It was a powerful visual that demonstrated how to instill a sense of pride among a constituency. Surely, the advertisement also resulted in an increase in applications for admission from women who shared similar aspirations.

20 Invite A Guest Speaker To Address Your Board Of Directors.

This technique isn't anything new. But, when was the last time you tried it? Every board runs into gridlock . And when that happens, consensus on a particular issue needs to be reached to overcome the gridlock. An outsider can act as a mediator and address the elements of agreement that both sides share on a particular issue. A guest speaker can also remind the board that it must act in the "best interest" of the organization. Even your directors get tired of hearing themselves talk. When the discussion of an issue becomes tiresome and repetitive, invite an outsider to address your board. Be sure your guest speaker is properly briefed about the board's composition — the backgrounds of board members, their particular expertise and their accomplishments as board members. It takes a skilled speaker to handle such an assignment, but it's worth the risk. After all, gridlock is not progress.

21 Appeal To The Self-interests Of Each Board Member.

As noble as we wish to be, most of us serve on a nonprofit board because we have a self-interest in doing so. Self-interest may not always be a primary factor for serving, but it's there. Increasingly, nonprofit boards are viewed by directors as a means to an end — bettering their network of contacts, increasing exposure to community leaders or building resumes for the next board they want to serve on. There's no problem with such reasons. There must be some benefit to directors for giving so much of their time.

In my own case, I serve as a trustee of Wadhams Hall Seminary College in upstate New York, where I graduated in 1972. Since I live in Florida and the college is in the uppermost part of New York state, I have an interest in traveling there four times a year to attend trustee meetings. I was born and raised in that part of New York. My mother, four siblings, relatives and many friends still live there. Thus, I get to see them at least annually, if not more. Prior to serving on the board, I visited home once every three years at the most.

Another reason for serving as a trustee is my desire to learn more about the needs and trends in the Roman Catholic Church regarding preparation of young men for the priesthood. What better way to stay current than being involved at the nucleus of such activity? During these meetings, I learn about other aspects of the church and my faith that would not be possible if I wasn't involved as a trustee. In return, however, Wadhams Hall has had my assistance in a major endowment campaign and presidential search, as well as general guidance on key issues. It's a win-win situation for the college and me.

22 Have Each Board Member Ask For A Gift.

Believe it or not, there are board members who have gone through their entire term without ever asking a prospect to give to the organization. How does this happen? Because the board allows it.

After you have successfully implemented a board giving policy (See number 15), you should assign each board member several prospects. The process of making "the ask" reminds board members of the importance of asking. It also provides them with the opportunity to learn firsthand what your donors and prospective donors think about your organization.

A main benefit of having board members actively asking for support is that it reduces the board's dependence on the staff to make the request. This keeps the emphasis where it belongs: volunteer to volunteer, not paid staff to volunteer.

Directors of nonprofit organizations should realize that people expect to be asked to give. More often than not, prospects will give when properly asked. People like to hear the message, "I need you." One thing is for certain, prospective donors won't feel needed if they are not asked. The best time to assign prospects to your board members is after they have made their own gift, not before. A basic principle of fund-raising is — make your own gift before you ask anyone else to give. This is of paramount importance when it comes to your board of directors. What kind of message are you sending if your directors ask for gifts to your cause when they haven't yet contributed? The obvious answer is that your cause isn't worthwhile; consequently, you won't be taken seriously.

23 Talk About Your Investments, Not Your Costs.

If you want to motivate your board of directors to advance the work of your organization, change your vocabulary from "budgeted dollars" to "investment dollars." Investing implies a return. Budgeted dollars are static. Pity the nonprofit executive whose board sees its role as that of twenty individual bean counters watching every nickel spent. It doesn't take much talent to be a budget cop who just sits there and says, "We must stay within the budget."

On the other hand, it does take talent to look at a situation and say, "If we invest these dollars in our marketing department's budget, we stand a reasonable chance of obtaining a return of 'x' dollars in return from the sale of products or services."

Directors of nonprofit organizations enjoy their role of holding the line on budgets. Executive directors are under pressure to advance the growth and development of the organization. This usually means coming up with new ideas and programs that require an investment of money, as well as some risk taking. Find a director who understands this concept and have him sell the idea to the rest of the board.

24 Research And Report The Potential For Giving.

Research capability exists today that development officers years ago could only dream of — actually determining the potential for giving within the donor base. Electronic screening, as it's called, is a marvelous high-tech tool that has proven itself even to the skeptics. Several firms are now providing prospect research/screening services to fundraising departments. These firms typically develop a profile of your donors based upon the information you provide them. The company then checks each name against public information and credit summary information they subscribe to. After thousands of analyses, they can calculate the giving potential for an individual donor in your database. Furthermore, they provide you with a dazzling report, which is separated into annual, capital and planned giving categories. Each prospect is listed according to their highest potential for giving to your organization. This rating becomes the suggested amount for your next request through the mail, over the telephone or in person.

The greatest benefit of this service is seen when the report is presented to your board or development committee. On several occasions, I have been with clients and watched the reaction of the members of the board of directors when they were told about the untapped potential that exists within their own database.

Prior to the use of electronic screening services, boards would speak negatively about the organization's potential for raising more money.

They didn't believe it was possible. They had only seen slight increases in giving from year to year and didn't understand that the fund-raising goal could be raised. With the use of electronic screening services, you change that perspective. The board members start saying things such as, "If all that money is out there, we had better start asking for it. Do we have enough staff to contact all those prospects? Maybe we should hire additional development staff."

Another way to demonstrate your potential for increased support is through the traditional capital campaign feasibility study. This is used strictly for a specific capital project such as construction of a new building. Typically, a fund-raising firm conducts a study consisting of fifty or more interviews with potential donors. The ensuing report provides you with an analysis of the potential for giving relative to your proposed goal. About fifty percent of these studies report great potential for a campaign. When that's the case, the study also serves as a motivator for the board to move ahead with a capital fund drive.

As the competition for charitable dollars increases, your board of directors must be persuaded with solid facts as to the potential for increased support. Once you have this evidence, it's much easier to engage the board in fundraising.

25 Besting The Other Guy.

Competition motivates everyone. No one really wants to be beaten regardless of the game being played. One of the first things you learn in Fund Raising 101 is the importance of campaign report meetings. Having a wall chart with the name of the division chair on the top and the running total of dollars raised for his division below says a lot about who is winning at securing contributions. My first job with the United Way made me a believer in the concept of "Besting The Other Guy." I saw mature professionals break out in a cold sweat for fear of placing last in these competitions. Sure, it was all in fun, but the competition was real. How often we fail to remember these simple lessons. It's time to use them again. They work.

26 Provide Approval And Positive Reinforcement When Merited.

Directors of boards need approval and positive reinforcement for their work. Not all volunteer directors have a high degree of confidence in themselves or the ability to raise funds. Many literally ask the agency executive, "How am I doing? Am I getting it right? Did I speak up too soon?" Obviously, these are the comments of a greenhorn director. However, seasoned directors of your board need approval, too, even for the smallest of achievements. Look for opportunities to provide sincere compliments to each director when warranted. Telephone them, write them, fax them, e-mail them or visit them. Be consistent in your praise. Make it a habit. Then, watch the confidence of your directors rise.

I often encourage clients to send a handwritten note along with any meeting summary or minutes that says something such as, "Glenn, I believe we had an excellent meeting. You certainly played a key role. Thank you for your leadership in directing the discussion." Or, you may want to be more formal and send a special cover letter. In either case, you are providing some well-deserved stroking.

27 Recognize and Reward Directors For Their Leadership.

Recently, I met with a banker whom I had recruited years ago to the board of directors of a public university foundation. During the course of the conversation, he told me that his bank had just contributed $10,000 to the university's foundation. He asked me if I thought that was a sizeable gift. I reminded him of the bank's humble beginnings just five years ago and said, "Yes, that is a serious gift for a bank of your size." He appreciated my affirmation of the bank's generosity.

Then he told me that he had not received any recognition for his time served on the foundation board and that little fuss was made over the bank's gift. Clearly, someone at the university had failed to recognize and reward this community banker for his gifts of time and money. He no longer intended to give again or be involved. In fact, he'd like to spend his time with another institution of higher education that has been cultivating him for membership on their board. Because he moved on, the university lost more than money. It missed the banker's expertise, leadership and, most importantly, his goodwill.

Recognition is so easy to provide. Why is it so

often overlooked? How much effort does it take to include the name of a director in your newsletter, honor roll of donors, press release or special mention at a luncheon or dinner meeting? Wall plaques, trophies, paperweights and letter openers are all examples of modest recognition devices. One important factor to keep in mind — be sure to spell the person's name right on these items.

28 Patronize Your Directors' Business. It's A Good Business Practice.

Every nonprofit board is comprised of business and professional people. Look around your own board. Chances are you have directors who own their own business — be it a car dealership, insurance agency, accounting firm or retail shop. The more successful your directors are in their businesses, the more they will have to contribute. Plus, their circle of influence will be much greater. We often overlook the importance of helping our directors succeed. After all, they spend a lot of their time helping your organization succeed.

I recall the time we had a surgeon on a university board. I did not need any surgery, so it wasn't likely that I could send any business his way. However, his wife owned and operated a bath works shop. It had everything you'd ever need in a bathroom. One day when I was between appointments, I stopped by her shop. She remembered me from the university functions she attended, so we proceeded to talk about how her surgeon husband was able to find the time to serve on our board. I made a modest purchase, wished her well and left. A few

weeks later, I saw her husband. He was so apprecia-
tive that I had stopped by, you would have thought
I had purchased the store's entire inventory. As a
successful surgeon, he and his wife did not need
my business to pay their monthly mortgage; however, they were both genuinely grateful for the
expression of interest.

29 Create A Written Paper Trail.

Another tactic that has worked for me is to send out a lot of correspondence. After you telephone a director, you have the additional opportunity of following up with a brief written communication. Again, it's the process here, following through, that's so important. You called, you discussed something and now you are sending (as promised) a written confirmation. Sounds so simple or trite; however, it builds confidence in the staff for being "on top of things." For example, attach a Post-It note to a previously mailed agenda with a hand-written note saying, "Looking forward to your report at the board meeting."

30 Fax Messages That Stand Out To Your Directors.

When the facsimile machine first came out, I envisioned having the equivalent of a Western Union Telegram machine in my office. Now **here** is a high-tech machine that screams out, "This message is important!" Ever notice how fax messages are given immediate attention by the office staff? The medium is definitely an attention-getter, especially when you include a cartoon from "The New Yorker" magazine or local newspaper that drives home a particular point.

The trick with fax messages is not to overdo it. Too many fax messages can pile up just like those pink telephone message slips. The fax is a great way to send last-minute and fast-breaking information to directors. If the person you are trying to contact has a voice-mail system, a fax message is a quick way to get around it. For example, you can fax a note to Mr. Carlton stating, "I'd like to call you today between 3 and 4 to discuss the meeting agenda. Are you available at that time?" It saves the time of going through gatekeepers, has a sense of urgency to it and shows that you're sensitive to his time.

31 Use Humor To Tell A Good Story.

Studies show that people retain more of what is said when humor is used. Hal Roach, the great Irish humorist, tells his audience that "laughing is good for you." It's hard to be anxious and tense while having a great laugh. Humor is being used more often as a communication tool in business. It has helped many executives keep their sanity during the turbulent times of corporate downsizing. Former president Ronald Reagan, who left

office as the oldest president, used humor to poke fun at himself, especially his age. He also used humor during press conferences to answer the press corps' nasty questions. The effect was always the same — people relaxed and became less serious.

Your board chair, executive director or any board member can do the same as Roach and Reagan. You don't have to be a pro to tell a good joke or story. Just remember your lines, especially the punch line. Here's one of my favorite stories that I tell right after being introduced. I don't recall where I read it, so proper credit is not possible. It is an effective story for demonstrating the importance of clear communication.

Edward R. Murrow, the legendary CBS News commentator, had a television show toward the latter part of his career called "Person To Person." It was a half-hour interview format with Murrow and his guest. On one particular show, Conrad Hilton, the great American industrialist and founder of the Hilton Hotel chain, discussed American capitalism and the economy of the day. At the end of the interview, Murrow asked Hilton if he would like to make a summary statement directly to the American people. Hilton turned and looked directly into the camera and said, "Yes. Please keep the shower curtain inside the tub."

I love this story for its practicality in setting the stage for a discussion on how to communicate your message. Here was a captain of American industry talking about a complicated business subject and in closing he makes a simple but practical request — don't make a mess. This story is an excellent example of effective communication that has helped me over the years in beginning my seminars by emphasizing to audiences that fund raising starts with good, clear communication.

If you are facing a tense board meeting, surprise everyone by starting out with a good story or joke to reduce everyone's stress.

32 Send Out A Press Release.

During my first staff job with the United Way of my hometown Utica, New York, I was struck by the importance that was placed on sending out press releases on the election of board members and appointments of campaign volunteers. I used to tease the public relations director that his pay-check depended upon how many of those releases were used by the media. Being brand new to the staff right out of college, I quickly learned that this exercise was a serious matter. People who volunteer their time to your cause want others to know of their involvement and what accomplishments the organization has made. This is especially true when volunteers are elected or appointed to key leadership positions.

Keep your press release simple. For example, "Jennifer Saunders, vice president of Marketing for Sun Resources Inc., was recently elected to a two-year term on the Board of Directors of the Houston Girl Scouts Council." Be sure to use the standard press release format of providing the name of a contact. This is usually the person who wrote the release or your spokesperson on this matter. Also, send a black-and-white photo, preferably provided by your board member. (Your office should make any necessary duplicates.) Be sure to send your release to trade publications within the director's industry or profession, your community newspapers and the weekly business section of the local papers, which often publish such information. Competition for space in major daily newspapers is keen and often limited to key executive appointments at major corporations, but smaller publications are eager to use well-written news releases.

Beware of the naysayers who discourage you from sending out such releases because they believe the media won't use it. Ignore them. Also, be sure to send a copy of the release to your board member before you send it out. Allow him or her to make corrections, but subtly let the member know that changes should be for correctness and political or personal sensitivities — not for rewriting or editing. It shows that your organization is proud to have a new member on your board and that you care about his or her visibility in the community as an up-and-coming business executive.

33 Entertain With A Message.

Local community theater groups are an untapped source of entertainment with a custom-made message for your board. Nearly every nonprofit organization has an annual meeting, which usually includes a noted guest speaker to rally the troops. Why not conduct a brief theatrical skit instead that conveys the same message that a guest speaker would have delivered? Live theater is exciting, fun, entertaining and adds a touch of class to your meeting. Whether your organization focuses on the homeless, youths, senior citizens, the environment or animals, the only limitation for crafting a twenty-minute skit is your imagination. Use the simple formula of introducing the subject, describing the problem/misery, demonstrating the solution and concluding with an emotional triumph.

Contact the director of your local theater, request a meeting and outline your needs. Negotiate a fair fee so there is a direct benefit to the theater as well. You are providing the theater with the opportunity to demonstrate its talent before your board, potential theatergoers themselves. A practice run should be held to anticipate any potential problems, such as space, sound or sightlines.

34 Motivate With A Video Movie Clip.

If you can't persuade a community theater group to assist you, show a brief scene from a movie. There are hundreds of movies with messages that entertain, delight and motivate. "Apollo 13," the true story of how close NASA came to losing three astronauts in space, has a great scene in which the flight director, played by Ed Harris, demands that a team be immediately assembled to figure out how to "put a square peg in a round hole" using only those materials the astronauts have on board their spaceship. The lesson learned? In tough situations, everyone on your board must pull together as a team and work the problem until they fix it. Team building is an important exercise in the development of nonprofit boards.

Comedy movies can serve a double purpose — humor and the lesson drawn from the clip. Movies such as "Father of the Bride" with Steve Martin, demonstrate how parents communicate on one level while their children are on another. Videos provide so many valuable lessons. When properly researched, planned and utilized, these visual treasures can enhance your meeting.

Most public libraries have extensive collections of videos for loan. The reference librarian just needs to know the subject matter or message you want to convey to your board. This can be cross referenced to the movie that best suits your situation.

Two great films that emphasize board involvement in decision making are "Wall Street" and "Barbarians At The Gate." While these are both examples of for-profit boards of directors in action, they do demonstrate the power of board leadership. Michael Douglas plays a CEO takeover expert in "Wall Street" and James Garner is the embattled CEO in "Barbarians At The Gate." There are plenty of clips in both movies that feature intense dialogue on issues of right and wrong.

35 Give Your Directors A Reading Assignment.

The Center for Nonprofit Boards in Washington D.C. has a catalog of excellent books, pamphlets and videos on a wide range of subjects important to directors of nonprofit boards, from "How To Be An Effective Board Member" to" Evaluating Your Board of Directors." These resources can be real eye-openers to board members when properly assigned by the chair. Purchase a set of these books; send one to each of your directors with a note from your chair requesting that directors read a particular chapter and come to the next board meeting prepared to discuss it. To get the discussion moving, the chair should provide his or her reflections first, then go around the room asking other directors for their thoughts. Everyone should have the chance to say something. After everyone is done, the chair should then summarize the meaning or message of what was said and point out how your organization can follow the advice and begin operating differently in the future.

36 Start Your Meeting With A Prayer.

Sometimes nonprofit organizations face problems that seem beyond any human solution. When that's the case, someone usually suggests it's time to pray. Prayer does make a difference. Studies indicate that patients who are ill and pray have a more positive attitude about overcoming their illness. Physicians welcome prayer as part of the recovery process. Similarly, starting your meetings with a prayer can also be helpful. By praying you are acknowledging the board's human limitations and its dependence upon a higher power. My heart goes out to those who have never experienced the power of prayer. There have been so many meetings I've begun over the years without having any idea as to how to fix a problem. Being a consultant is often a humbling experience, because you quickly find out you don't have the answers to every problem that comes up. Prayers before meetings usually take the form of a request for guidance or insight. They usually have a calming affect on those present. As my friend Father Ralph W. Beiting, founder of the Christian Appalachian Project, says, "If you are doing God's work, he will provide whatever help you need in doing so. Just ask through prayer."

37 Always Arrive Ahead Of Time For Appointments.

Surveys today indicate that the number one thing most people wish they had was more time in the day — more time to spend with their family, to exercise, to read and learn, or just to relax. Respect for another person's time is an important factor in today's nonprofit world. Directors of nonprofit organizations are volunteers who give freely of their time. Staff and fellow directors themselves must understand that there is no excuse for wasting a volunteer's time. To do so is the equivalent of the farmer who lost his barn to fire. His neighbors decided to have a barn raising, but couldn't begin because the farmer was too busy with other tasks. You don't keep an army of volunteers waiting with hammers and saws to build a new barn. Never be on time for an appointment with a director — be ahead of time! You will be more appreciated and effective in your relationships with directors.

Carlton Ketchum, a founder of the legendary fund-raising firm Ketchum Inc., used to instruct his consultants to always be fifteen minutes early for any meeting with volunteers. His rationale was that it would be insulting to waste it. That's good advice every nonprofit executive should follow.

38 Keep The Board Informed By Sending Reports.

Take advantage of our high-tech society by using the many information systems that are at your disposal. Written reports can be produced easier

and faster with desk-top, lap-top and on-line computers. As the Internet and World Wide Web increase in usage, more of us will use this high-tech library to generate reports on subjects of interest to our cause, be it finding a cure for cancer or keeping our rivers and streams free of pollution. I can hear you now saying, "But my directors won't take the time to read the report." I admit there's always that chance; however, keeping directors motivated means keeping their interest level high. The more information they have on a particular aspect of your organization's work, the better informed they will be as directors. Making the effort to provide this information says that you expect directors to be informed and to do their homework.

Most directors will take the time to read your reports if they are serious about their duty as directors. To ensure that your reports are read, provide a one-page summary. Make the first sentence an attention getter. For example, "This summary explains how a Boy Scout Council in Texas increased its membership base by 150 percent in ten months." Then provide the highlights. Graphs and pictures make the information easier to digest. You could include a footnote telling the reader that they can request more detailed information.

Notice during your next board meeting how some directors will have read what you sent them and others did not. This in itself creates a little internal board competition as to who is on top of the issues.

By sending such reports, you are demonstrating that you care about your directors in fulfilling their roles. The better informed they are on issues facing your organization, the greater their performance as directors.

39 Plan Meetings To The Last Detail.

How often have you heard it said after a board of directors meeting, "That was one of our best meetings ever"? What is really being said is, "Someone carefully planned and orchestrated the meeting from start to finish." I call this, "The meeting before the meeting tactic." To start, a board of directors meeting should never be announced until those calling it know exactly what end result they are expecting from the meeting. Otherwise, you allow for an unstructured atmosphere that can turn into a series of mini-speeches or sermons on how to keep costs down or why you should undertake a new special event fund raiser.

Have you planned the meeting agenda and anticipated how the discussion will go? Have the directors who are expected to carry the discussion been properly briefed? And are they ready to move ahead? Have you anticipated any objections that might arise and how and who will answer these? Do you have the necessary votes needed to get your agenda items approved?

In addition to these considerations, you should consider this checklist:

1. Meeting date — What's the best date for the

largest attendance? Call each director to find out.

2. What's the agenda?

3. Is the location convenient for all involved?

4. Has an advance meeting notice gone out with an agenda?

5. Has a reminder notice been sent two days prior to the actual meeting date?

6. Has a telephone call been made to those who haven't said they plan to attend?

7. Is the meeting room arranged comfortably and to encourage group discussion?

8. Is the heat or air conditioning working properly?

9. Is there sufficient and easy parking and building access for everyone?

10. Has someone been assigned to greet directors and assist them as they arrive?

11. Have copies of all handouts been made and properly placed at each director's seat?

12. Do directors have name placards? If so, have their names been spelled right?

A well-planned meeting begins with a limited agenda, usually no more than five items of business. Always begin the meeting with those items that can be dealt with in the least amount of discussion before getting into the more substantial items which require in-depth discussion or debate. Make sure the chair of the board moves the agenda along, demonstrating how the board is making progress by handling each item completely before moving on to the next. This builds a sense of teamwork. The chair should also frame the discussion of the major agenda items and offer brief opening remarks of his or her own before inviting comments by other directors. Once the discussion begins, the chair should keep a firm hand on the meeting rudder, always steering the discussion forward and discouraging remarks that are not pertinent to the subject at hand. That's why a good chair says things such as, "Thank you, Charles, for sharing that with us; however, I'd prefer you bring that up later under new business. Right now, I'm limiting the remarks to our annual audit."

Good meetings don't just happen. They are planned. The better they are planned, the greater the sense of accomplishment. As Benjamin Franklin said, "By failing to prepare, you prepare to fail."

40 Be Open To Counterpoints Of View.

Most people are threatened by strong opinions that are different from their own. Being open to counterpoints of view is one way to assure you are striving for the right solution to a particular problem. How often have you heard this comment dur-

ing a board meeting, "We've tried that; we've done that; it doesn't work"? This can be quite discouraging to an executive who is trying to tackle a project or problem in a new fashion. I know from my own experience as a trustee of my alma mater that this attitude can put a real damper on new initiatives. In fact, most of us tend to avoid solutions to problems that are out of the ordinary or slightly different from the standard approach. As a nonprofit executive, you must set the tone for honest dialogue through example. This means you must be open to new ideas yourself.

Sometimes, a problem facing your board may be too controversial to begin a discussion of an issue without preliminary preparation. If this is the case, begin by having a brainstorming session. The rules for brainstorming are simple. Everyone gets the chance to say something, but no one is allowed to criticize. Each person must improve on what the previous person said. Only after everyone has spoken is the board allowed to evaluate the ideas put forth. By postponing the critical review of comments, you are creating an atmosphere of creative problem-solving.

Creative solutions can only be fostered in an open environment. If your board of directors is in a rut, maybe you should ask this question, "Can we agree that there may be a better way and discuss new approaches without making immediate judgements as to whether or not they will work? We'll keep at this until we agree we have a solution."

41

Plan For Fun And Make Fun The Plan.

In the 1980's, I was fortunate to have a special donor at the University of Central Florida where I began the annual President's Circle

Dinners. The dinner was by invitation only to those who had contributed a minimum of $1,000 the prior year to the President's Circle. It was the president's way of thanking and publicly recognizing contributors to the university. A special reception was always held prior to the dinner at the home of our major sponsor. This donor contributed the cost of hiring world-famous speakers, such as Henry Kissinger, William F. Buckley and Helmut Schmidt. Only a handful of contributors and special guests were invited to the pre-dinner social. During the third year of our program, I asked our "angel," Mr. Georges C. St. Laurent, Jr., why he gave so generously of his time and money. His response to my question was, "Because I am having fun." That was in the early eighties. In mid-year of 1996, I caught up with Mr. St. Laurent on the West Coast where he now resides. We recalled over drinks all of the planning that went into these events. How his lovely wife Toodie was such a gracious hostess and perfectionist in planning the pre-dinner receptions with the speakers at their home. How William F. Buckley played the piano and how Dr. Henry Kissinger enjoyed the bar's huge built-in aquarium. Before I could utter a word, Mr. St. Laurent reminded me again why he was so generous and involved in this recognition program. He said, "Jim, it was all so much fun."

Never underestimate the power of fun when trying to motivate a member of your board. Professional fund raisers and nonprofit executives should remember that they are "arrangers of experiences" for your volunteers. This means you have the ability to orchestrate activities that have a special purpose, while simultaneously creating a memorable experience for volunteers. It has been sixteen years since I started the President's Circle Dinner program, but I still run into people who mention their fond memories of that event.

When you consider all of the pressures facing your directors today in their own personal or professional lives, having fun is a welcome relief. Make it your goal to arrange some fun for your board.

42 Keep Confidences Confidential.

Most board proceedings deal with sensitive, confidential matters. These occasions should be viewed as "tests" for both the staff and other directors who are obligated to keep confidences. Confidential matters among nonprofit boards usually revolve around human or financial resource issues, such as the salary negotiations with a new executive or the purchase of property for a new building site. The minute a board of directors is into the arena of confidentiality, directors become quite serious, tension increases, and everyone is worried about a leak. This is the time when the integrity and reputation of directors and staff is really on the line. A nonprofit board must be able to periodically conduct its business with the veil of secrecy. It has the right to expect those privy to sensitive information to keep confidences. When important business of a confidential nature is successfully conducted in confidence, directors of the board feel a double sense of accomplishment. They will be even more eager to tackle tough issues in the future because they have developed a sense of confidence among one another.

During my time at one major university, I recall

the board of directors having several closed-door sessions regarding a serious problem in the athletic department. A few days after the board meeting, a staff person privy to the minutes must have leaked information to the press. This public disclosure embarrassed the entire board, which then openly fought with each other thereafter. The press had a field day. The university's proceedings made it into the pages of "The New York Times." Eventually, the person responsible for the leak was discovered and terminated. Keeping a tight lip is also a way to keep your job.

"Once the toothpaste is out of the tube, it's difficult to put it back in."
— H.R. Halderman

---

43 Pick Up The Telephone And Call.

I must confess to having been influenced by Peter Falk who played the part of a detective in the television show, "Columbo." Detective Columbo, a bumbling sleuth, pretends he doesn't always know the answer to his questions. Imitating him has served me well over the years in working with directors of nonprofit boards. Like Columbo, I must admit to telephoning many of them over the years to quiz them about a matter I already had the answer for. Oftentimes, it's just to confirm an appointment, remind them of a meeting, check something out on an upcoming agenda — regardless, I invent reasons to stay in touch. Why? Because people are so busy today that you have to "be in their face" if you want to keep their attention and focus on your cause. If you recall, Columbo was always in touch with his "suspects." Often, he would appear unannounced at the most inopportune time, asking questions in his own charming way. If you were the target of his suspicion, you just knew this "gumshoe" wasn't going away until he got what he wanted from you. Like Columbo, be a pest, but a pleasant one.

44 Attend Your Directors Events. They Attend Plenty Of Yours.

Much like patronizing a director's business, you should always accept an invitation to attend any event a director is hosting, whether a personal holiday gathering or a grand opening of a new store. Directors sweat the details too when they host an event. They know how many invitations were sent out, who replied or who showed up. When you receive an invitation by a director of your board, be one of the first to send back your RSVP. Once at the event, be sure you personally say "hello" or "good-bye" to the host so that your attendance is noted. Why take the time to attend if you are not going to make your presence known? Directors give you a lot of their time; you should make time for them, too. By doing so, you will become a reliable guest, someone they can depend on when invited.

45 Be Available At All Times.

With today's communications technology, there is no excuse for not being available to your board of directors at all times. Electronic mail, portable

telephones, fax machines, personal pagers and voice mail make it possible to be reached wherever you are. Once again, your volunteer directors are giving freely of their time. Thus, they don't expect to spend a lot of their time hunting you down or waiting for you to return their calls. When they do call, they want to reach you right then or just as soon as you are available — day or night.

If your office is set up in the traditional way with a receptionist answering all incoming calls, be sure instructions are left to put any directors' calls through immediately. Never keep a director waiting. Directors should have every number they need to reach you printed on a special card — direct extension number, home number, mobile number, pager number and fax number. Quick and easy communication between directors and staff keeps the process of managing a nonprofit moving smoothly.

46 Pop Some Popcorn. Smell The Flavor.

We all know the irresistible smell of popcorn. Provide a freshly popped bag to each director as he or she enters the meeting. Postpone the start of the meeting for ten minutes to give everyone a chance to indulge in this universal snack. Watch how such a tasty treat adds levity and livens up your meeting. Have you ever met anyone who didn't enjoy freshly made popcorn? You might want to combine this suggestion with number 34 — when showing a video clip to make a key point.

47 Remind Directors That They Can Make A Difference.

One of the main reasons volunteers become board members is because they want to make a difference in society. Directors want to be part of the solution to the problems of the homeless, the fight against cancer or the clean-up of the environment. It is not unusual for a director to mention that they have watched a particular agency struggle over the years. Rather than complain from the sidelines, they decided to jump in and become a part of the solution. None of us wishes to leave things the way we found them. We all want to leave a legacy. It's important to remind directors that they are the critical difference in the work of your organization. They do make it possible to meet your mission, advance your agenda, accomplish your goals and make life better for those you serve. There are more than a million nonprofit boards in the country today. The successful ones are comprised of directors who see themselves as making a difference. The next time you reach a milestone in your organization, announce this success and remind your directors that they made the critical difference.

48 Include Spouses Or Significant Others.

One mistake nonprofit executives consistently make is underestimating the motivating power of a director's spouse or significant other. Remember, volunteer directors give freely of their time. The more time they give your organization, the less time they are spending with their businesses, families and spouses. The expenditure of this time must be viewed by the spouses as valuable. The best way to show how time is being well spent is to include the spouses or significant others of your directors as often as possible in your organization's meetings and events. For example, if you have an annual meeting, do you invite guests or limit attendance to directors only? Create occasions so that you can include the spouse. The more the spouses and significant others are involved, the more encouragement they will give to your directors, provided, of course, they are sold on your organization.

49 Spell The Directors' Names Right.

Don't laugh. It happens all the time. Rosters, name placards, programs and annual reports generally include a listing of your board of directors. You know what happens. A director picks up the publication, looks for his or her name before reading anything else and discovers it's spelled wrong. Make sure you personally check the spelling of the names of your directors on all of your written materials before they are printed. Also, insist that the staff double check your work. Never let letters, reports, honor rolls or brochures go out with board members' names misspelled. Always assume that if any name is misspelled, it will probably be a member of your board of directors or worse yet, the board chair.

50 Strive To Be A Generous Person.

If you want directors of your board to be generous with their time and money, then be an example of generosity yourself. Be generous in thought, word and deed. How can you expect to have a giving board if you are not a giving, caring person yourself? Do you think generously of your board, staff and donors? Do you use generous words? Do you practice generous acts? Do you contribute to your cause and others? Imagine how silly you look if you head a nonprofit organization that is heavily dependent on contributions, and you are seen as a tightwad. If you want your directors to be generous, you must practice generosity yourself. By setting this example, others will imitate you.

The late Dick Wilson, a former president of the National Society of Fund Raising Executives (NSFRE), was one of the most generous people I've known — a wonderful, warm, gentle, caring and giving individual. Each year, after making his personal contribution to the society, the United Way, his church and other charities, Dick did something quite extraordinary. He would set aside $1,000 for additional requests for his support. Throughout the year, he would evaluate the numerous mail appeals he received. He would read every one of them. Then, he sent five or ten dollars to each of them until the $1,000 was gone. It later occurred to me that in his capacity as president of NSFRE he could say to most members of the society, "I contribute to your organization." That extra $1,000 was probably a stretch for Dick; however, I believe it was one of the most generous acts of giving I've ever seen and it set an example his colleagues and I will never forget.

Index of Subjects

Accessibility of nonprofit executive	101,102	Lists	43
Appointments of directors	85	Making a difference	104
Assignments for directors	25,26	Meeting details	88,89,90
Board giving	44,45,46	Mission statement	17,18
Board retreat	19,20,21,22	Movie clips	81,82
Board solicitation	60,61	Organizational Assessment	37,38
Budgeted dollars	62	Organizational values	47,48
Case for support	49,50,51	Patronize directors	71,72
Competition among the board	66	Plan	15,16
Confidences, confidentiality	96,97	Policy on board giving	44,45,46
Correct spelling of names	106	Popcorn levity	103
Correspondence	73	Positive reinforcement	68
Counter points of view	91,92	Post-retreat follow-up	23,24
Directors' events	100	Prayer	84
Directors' expectations	13,14	Press Release	78,79
Directors' pride	54,55	Reading Assignment	83
Elevator speech, case	49,50,51	Recognition	69,70
Expertise of directors	32,33	Reports	86,87
Fax Messages	74	Researching giving potential	63,64,65
Fun	39,93,94,95	Self-interests	58,59
Generosity	107,108	Similar organization	40
Guest speakers	56	Spouses	105
Humor	75,76,77	Telephone use	98
Investment dollars	62	Theatrical uses	80
Job description for directors	28,29	Upward mobility	30,31
Know your directors	41,42	Vision statement	17,18
Leadership of directors	34,35,36	Volunteer calendar	52,53

Donovan Management, Inc.

Donovan Management is a Florida-based consulting firm that provides philanthropic managment, revenue enhancement and training services to nonprofit and corporate clients. Established in 1986, the firm has assisted over 100 clients in the United States and the Caribbean.

Summary of Services

Management Consulting
Strategic Planning
Assessment
Studies
Project Management

Revenue Enhancement
Cost Reduction Reviews
Fund Raising
Earned Income Strategies
Investment Strategies

Training
Client Seminars
Major Gift Solicitation
Retreat Facilitation
Conference Speaking

Corporate Philanthropy *
Volunteer Programs
Matching Gift Programs
Corporate Giving
Cause Related Marketing
Exxecutive Placement

* For Profit Section

For a copy of our services brochure, please call 407-366-8340 or write us at Donovan Management, P.O. Box 195068, Winter Springs, FL 32719.

For More Copies Of This Book

or

Take The Fear Out of Asking For Major Gifts

Call 1-800-247-3023*

or write

Donovan Management, Inc.
P.O. Box 195068
Winter Springs, FL 32719

Quantity Discounts Available

* A dedicated book order number only.

About The Author

James A. Donovan is author of the best-selling book, "Take The Fear Out Of Asking For Major Gifts." He is President of Donovan Management, Inc., a Florida-based consulting firm that provides philanthropic management, revenue enhancement and training services to nonprofit and corporate clients. Since its establishment in 1986, the firm has assisted over 100 clients in the United States and the Caribbean.

A twenty-five-year career veteran in philanthrophy, Donovan has become a nationally recognized lecturer in major gift fund raising and training. He has presented at three international conferences for the National Society of Fund Raising Executives and dozens of its chapters from Orlando to Oregon, as well as for such national organizations as the American Red Cross, American Cancer Society and the American Diabetes Association.

His articles, book reviews and commentary on philanthropy have been published by "Metropolitan Universities," "CASE Currents," "Chronicle of Philanthrophy," "Fund Raising Management Magazine" and "Resources," the firm's corporate newsletter.

He and his wife, Janet Donovan — to whom this book is dedicated — have two daughters, Kelly and Katie. They reside in Central Florida along with Bailey and Casey, their cat and Golden Retriever.